THE MAGNITUDE OF
MY SUBLIME EXISTENCE

SELIMA HILL

THE MAGNITUDE OF MY SUBLIME EXISTENCE

BLOODAXE BOOKS

ISBN: 978 1 78037 305 8

First published 2016 by
Bloodaxe Books Ltd,
Eastburn,
South Park,
Hexham,
Northumberland NE46 1BS.

www.bloodaxebooks.com
For further information about Bloodaxe titles
please visit our website or write to
the above address for a catalogue.

Supported by
**ARTS COUNCIL
ENGLAND**

Cover design: Neil Astley & Pamela Robertson-Pearce.

Printed in Great Britain by Bell & Bain Limited, Glasgow, Scotland, on
acid-free paper sourced from mills with FSC chain of custody certification.

To the Woman with the Long Black Hair
who may or may not want to be dedicated to
but to whom I am going to dedicate this anyway

CONTENTS

A bird does not sing because it has an answer
but because it has a song

CHINESE PROVERB

Cup

I don't know how they do it. And what's more,
it looks so easy for them. As for me,

I go to pieces like a little cup
made of sores nobody must touch.

Car

Because I'm always scared of being touched
I run away at the slightest thing

and when I run away I get lost
but as I always feel lost anyway

it doesn't make much difference, not to me,
until I'm found or hit by a car.

Lily

They might as well ask the glass lily
inside the glass paperweight to talk to them;

I can barely tell who they are,
far less what they want or how to talk to them:

I've no idea that doctors of all sizes
are being called; that some will prevail.

My Fist

I'm sitting on a bed by a wall,
washed and dressed and fed by who knows who,

and squeezing in my fist a rubber zebra
the size and texture of a little thumb

to shelter him from being dazzled by
the magnitude of my sublime existence.

Blossom

It feels like a dream of how it should be
when everything is not a dream but true

and nobody can stop me and the corridor
is shimmering like blossom on elastic.

Please don't interrupt me. I can't bear it.
I'm not that kind of person any more.

My New Home

I like the way no one's very friendly
and there isn't really anything to do;

I like the candlewick, I like the fruit-bowls
that no one seems to bother to use;

I like the way the doctors and the nurses
never seem to know what's going on;

I even like the woman who can't see,
who stubs her cigarettes out on her thumbs,

and most of all the fact we're all locked in
and everyone is here to enjoy themselves.

Eel

Actually, I'ld rather be an eel
and glide along in silence through the eel grass

and never have to touch, for example,
kiwifruit – I pray they don't have kiwifruit! –

or other people's hair, but the doctor
wants me to be human, and to talk.

Dr J

When Dr J. touches me I scream
and when I scream I scream as loud as possible

and everybody looks kind of scared
which seems a shame because it's only me.

Torpor

Torpor makes us shrivel up like cabbages
that might as well be white they're so blue,

the white of people sitting in the snow
who can't remember how to get back up again.

The Day-room

The day-room is for people who are dressed,
for people people chat to, and dare touch,

but not for me, as silent as a fire alarm
whose silence is a kind of thwarted ringing.

Sleet

If a nurse or patient gets too close
they glitter for a moment then dissolve

and soon I see the ward itself dissolve,
the yellow walls disintegrate like sleet,

until I can no longer make out
even my familiar round fruit-bowl.

The Word Zebra

If they come to see me I must speak
and look at them and let myself be cared for.

Being loved is good. It's what we want.
But secretly I prefer spelling.

Shame

I ought to be ashamed of myself –
and when I am I'll know I'm feeling better –

but now if someone's trying to be kind
all I do is shut my eyes and scream at them.

Nurse P.

She's prodding me and telling me to move
and brush my hair and put some make-up on.

She's very tall which doesn't feel right.
And also I don't like the way her name is spelt.

When she comes and stands beside my bed
my orders are to smile but I don't.

Drink my tea, eat my food, *smile*.
It can't be that impossible. *Do it*.

Being ill is all very well
but when I'm ill I don't know what I'm doing

or where my mouth has gone I'm meant to do it with.
Being ill is not for the faint-hearted!

Heaven

My brain is like a heaven full of larks
that lay their eggs in hollows in the ground

where any minute now a large cow
is liable to accidentally step on them.

Owls

Is it only me that isn't normal?
Or could it be that everybody else

is thinking they're not so-called 'normal' too?
Are we being dreamt in some way?

Are we being dreamt by a dreamer
who can't or won't console or even contact us;

who dreams of what she dreams must be a watchtower
where women stand with gonks and watch for owls?

Linoleum

If it gets too noisy I pass out
and people find me lying on the floor

demonstrating how to be linoleum
by flattening my hands against my ears.

Thousands of Miniature Dachshunds
from All Over the World

Thousands of miniature dachshunds from all over the world
suspended on meathooks in specially-designed freezers

and thousands of dead chinchillas wrapped in hair-nets
and thousands of duck-legs and thousands of dead pigs

and thousands of beautiful boys in dark woods
and hundreds and thousands of sluices and mysterious
        heliosheaths

are very sad but not as sad as somebody
sitting on her bed counting pills.

Doctor D.

Although he thinks he touches whom he touches,
and I myself sit tight as if it's true,

I'm actually someone else entirely
who sleeps in fins and spends the whole night swimming.

Treatment Day Afternoon

Arranged in rows in dressing-gowns by nurses,
we lie entranced as if we can't move,

as if we are submerged in warm mud –
until the nurses come and move us on again.

Me and K.

When everyone's asleep except the two of us
I watch her as she feels for her lighter

and, leaning her enormous body forward,
scorches the tips of her fingers,

and sometimes I imagine that she's watching me,
although I know she's blind; and I can't talk.

A Person with a Saw

When I want to think, I line things up –
like lining up these words, for example;

and when I'm dead a person with a saw
can saw my head in half and make two bowls

and shake, or pour, then line up, toffees in them
and then the person with the saw can eat them.

Wall

Day and night my fingers scratch the wall
to try and find a nook or a cranny

in order to escape through from a world
to which I have become too proud to turn.

Lounger

When the handsome doctor walks towards me
I get the feeling that a lounger gets

when somebody comes along and shakes it
although he knows it's *never going to work*.

The Woman with Long Black Hair

Late last night someone was brought in
I only caught a glimpse of – long black hair

and hairy legs she kicked the doctor with
whose smell she'll now be smelling of herself.

Dr G.'s Ears

Dr G. is poring over me
with giant ears, like the ears of God

Who's far too far away for me to talk to Him,
or even wave to Him, so I don't.

B. and the Evangelist

This morning an evangelist appeared
and wheeled her away in her wheelchair

and now she's back, *on her own two feet*,
and staggering around like a colt.

As the man is packing up her things
an orderly bursts into tears.

The Woman in the Bed Next to Mine

I wish I didn't know about the razor
the woman in the bed next to mine

is hiding at the back of her locker
beside a little mirror, also banned;

I wish it was OK to ask the registrar
to squeeze my chest so tight I can't breathe –

and I wish I had a brain like a goose,
that tells her what to do and she does it.

Behind the Yellow Curtains

When someone stumbles, as they often do,
and beg for help, and jerk their pasty arms,

I hide myself behind the yellow curtains.
Apart from that, I never go anywhere.

The Villa

First there is the sound of someone running
and then a scream and then the sound of porters
and someone being marched off to The Villa

where women who refuse to be women
disappear until they can behave themselves
or, if they can't, until the end of time.

Zebra

Its rubber brain is happy being rubber
and doesn't understand a word they say

and never has to worry about sanity
and what the point of sanity might be.

Silver

No one likes to be here when she's eating.
(Would you call it 'eating'? – being fed? –

until she's gained enough to go back home,
only to return a few weeks later

on a drip, her body almost silver…)
I like the word *silver*. Don't look.

I also like the fact we have no visitors –
unless you count the porters as visitors.

ECT

Like owls in zoos forgetting how to fly,
the women sleeping off their ECT

alternately remember and forget
where they are and where they want to be

and what they want to do – which is kill themselves,
or, in the case of owls in zoos, fly.

The Singers

Someone new is propped inside the side-room.
The tiny purple hands and bandaged wrists
grip a pack of Russian cigarettes.
She glares at us and we glare back.
Sister says to *move* but we don't.

At night I see her body shine with scars –
the woman who will later break my heart
with stories of the deaths in distant settlements
of women who could do no more than sing...
But that was later. Now I ignore her.

Torpid Ewes

When they used to ask me all those questions
and when I didn't answer, they would shake me

but here they just ignore me and stupidity
settles on our beds and chairs like snow

settling on the backs of torpid ewes,
enfolding all we have and all we need.

The Heiress

She hangs her head in sorrow like a horse
that understands there's nothing it can do,

but once I thought I saw what looked like smiles
playing round her perfect lips like cherubim.

(Cherubim are sometimes known as cherubs
but I prefer the Hebrew *cherubim*.)

Women Look So Ugly When They're Bored

Women look so ugly when they're bored,
lolling on their beds but we don't mind.

Someone's begging for a drink of water.
Outside in the world normal women

are stepping into showers with their lovers
and getting wetter than the wettest ducks.

Woman in a Nightdress

When it's time to leave they turn and wave
but the woman doesn't wave back.

They find it is impossible to feed her,
although they are her parents, unfortunately.

Lettuces

Outside in the sun a million lettuces
are springing up like tennis balls but here,

on the seventh floor, behind thick curtains,
no one stirs or even dreams of stirring:

we sit in rows like cushions doing nothing,
or rolling over on our backs like fish;

we marvel at the swifts or are they swallows
and go to sleep at all the wrong times.

Boa

All I want to do is wet my hair
and stay like that until I feel better:

I cannot tolerate being brushed against
by even my own hair. I used to scream

but now I know I need to find some water
and hide my head inside it like the ostrich

that also gets the urge to hide its head –
but what about its eyes in all that sand?

It's ticklier than its feathers! By the way,
the ostrich knows quite well it's not invisible,

that people come from far and wide in charabancs
expressly to admire its big brown feet.

Woman in a Blanket

Behind the yellow door of the side-room
the nurses can be heard setting up.

There's somebody inside, in a blanket,
close to tears and soaked to the bone.

In time I will befriend her – later on,
when I will have learnt to be kind.

The Lounge

Visitors call it the lounge
but it's not 'the lounge', it's the day-room,

but, day or night, it make no difference to us,
we might as well be locked in a *Departure Lounge*

but not a real Departure Lounge, obviously –
nobody in here is going *anywhere*,

or if we are we do not want to know,
far less have it stuffed in our faces.

The Letter E

Although we barely look at one another,
let alone smile, like they tell us to,

we care for one another – for example,
we help each other with our suicides,

or let each other sleep, or, in my case,
alternately repeat to myself

zebra with a short and then a long 'e',
the former the original Congolese.

The End of the World

No one knows the first thing about her
but I despise her anyhow, for everything –
for being clean, as if her life depended on it;
for sitting in the day-room drinking Lucozade
and thinking it's the end of the world

or not the end of the world, I can't remember;
for wanting to be friends -- *excuse me,*
never mention friends in here, OK ? –
but when I get too bored of despising her
I'll go and talk her through her various pills.

What to Die of and What Not to Die of

When everybody else is asleep
and nothing can be heard on the ward
except the distant laughter of the night staff,

the woman in the bed next to mine
likes to come and chat to me (why me?)
On she goes about the same old thing –

what to die of and what not to die of,
when and how to do it – all the time
cheerfully sitting on my ankles.

Blood Tests

I recognise the doctors by their shoes
(remember I can't recognise faces —
don't ask me why I can't but I can't):

they snuffle here and there like small animals
that live in pairs underneath the tables
and couldn't care two hoots about Blood Tests.

The Lady with the Trolley

When I swim nobody can hug me –
when I *used to swim*, I should say –

and when the lady with the trolley comes
I walk away because she's got no lake.

Sister's Favourite

When Sister comes and blows her a kiss
Sister's Favourite blinks, and Sister smiles:

after all, she is Sister's Favourite.
Or actually one of Sister's two favourites.

Lice

To run about all day with nothing on,
to have no name, to be completely silent,

to feel free to hop inside my hair
and find a greasy curl or a root

in which to stimulate each other's tiny body-parts,
to never not be normal must be bliss.

African Violets

The tall consultant looks me in the eye.
He thinks I want to die and I do.

I want to die and see what happens next.
It's got be more fun than staying here!

I never want to see another fruit-bowl
or potbound African Violet again.

Swallow

When I'm being touched it's hard to swallow
and when it's hard I 'lapse into sign'.

(By 'swallow' I mean swallow not the swallow
one of which *does not a summer make*;

by 'being touched' I mean being brushed against.
Being squeezed is absolutely fine.)

A Visit from the Chaplain

Mirrors aren't allowed and we've forgotten
who we are or even what we look like.
We see our veins of course but not our faces
but anyway who cares about our faces:
we can look like anything we want!

I may be wrong but yesterday a visitor
popped his head in with a bunch of flowers –
and looked as if he couldn't believe his eyes!
Women are so ugly! As we know.
Our inner beauty fails to shine through.

Are Dachshunds Ever White? Can Zebras Swim?

Are dachshunds ever white? Can zebras swim?
Can never having kissed one's own mother,

shameful though it is, be forgiven?
And late at night when everyone's asleep

does the doctor close the office door
and sit the little nurses on his knee?

And do the nurses grab him by the shoulders
and kiss him till their mouths begin to bleed,

cursing, as they kiss him, both the doctor
and us, his dumb, pig-headed devotees?

Strange Hats

Cleanliness is next to who or what
and who has special needs and who has not

and *godliness* is what exactly anyhow
and all that glitters is not which or why

and asking normal people normal questions
is never going to work and strange hats,

especially bobble-hats, will be removed,
and hats that have been starched will be transmogrified.

Tranquillity

Like cats in boxes who no longer mew,
it's not as if we care because we don't;

and also, we're not 'lazy', we are *tranquillised*,
and neither are we 'bored', we are *suffering*.

Marmalade

I know they think I think I'm very clever
but all I want to do is be like them –

by 'them' I mean *those who are happy*,
not my fellow inmates, obviously.

I'm working on it though. As a start,
I've trained myself to tolerate marmalade.

Useless Facts About Pigs

I've got to go and eat in the canteen,
and let the nurses walk me to the lawn;

I've got to join the others in the day-room
and sign up for O.T. I refuse.

I've got to *just get used to it*, she says.
She's sick of useless facts about pigs,

zebras, dachshunds, jellyfish, old cats;
she's sick and tired of *the whole lot of them*.

Twenty Years Ago for One Tick

It's hard to feel better but I do.
I know I do because I feel bad

for having been unkind to my mother
when she herself was always kind to me.

The trouble is the thought of being better
terrifies me and I lose my nerve,

and all because my mother *took her eyes off me*
twenty years ago *for one tick*.

Various New Tests

Now that I am no longer mute
they're testing me and this is what I say:

'Do I press the black one or the white one?'
Either, says the doctor, but the social worker,

although she knows 'either' is correct,
answers 'white' to simplify it for me.

Tomatoes

I've noticed other people like tomatoes;
I myself prefer simple facts –

the fact of my existence, for example;
quadruples; facts about euphoria –

facts that *never fail to exist*,
that *never change*, and therefore are a comfort to me;

Showing off? Why would I do that?
I'm no more quoting facts to impress them

than someone giving birth is giving birth
in order to impress a passing lugworm.

And please don't even think of trying to tell me
there's more to life than backstroke when there's not.

What a Beetle Sounds Like When It's Old

On my own for the first time,
the curious thought suddenly occurs to me

that I can kill a stranger. Just like that.
She's in the park. I can hear her breathing.

She sounds like an exhausted little beetle…
Now thinking of the beetle has endeared her to me!

Swimming-pool

Everybody seems to be so busy –
playing tennis, making new friends,

even with the swimming-pool attendant
who stares at me as if I've just been born.

Little does he know I haven't seen
a car, a child, glass, for five long months,

far less such a thing as a *swimming-pool*,
with or without a swimming-pool attendant.

Fruit-bowls

The sun that shines on me will not be shining
on the women I have left behind

half-asleep beside their empty fruit-bowls
with only dust-mites there to hold their hands.

Among the Jellyfish

Freed from being frozen in insanity
like someone's frozen wedding bouquet,

free at last, I'm stretched out in the sea,
gliding in my fins among the jellyfish

that always look so mad you can't help loving them
while praying that their frilly arms won't sting.

Selima Hill grew up in a family of painters on farms in England and Wales, and has lived by the sea in Dorset for the past 30 years. She won first prize in the Arvon/*Observer* International Poetry Competition with part of *The Accumulation of Small Acts of Kindness* (1989), one of several extended sequences in *Gloria: Selected Poems* (Bloodaxe Books, 2008). *Gloria* includes work from *Saying Hello at the Station* (1984), *My Darling Camel* (1988), *A Little Book of Meat* (1993), *Aeroplanes of the World* (1994), *Violet* (1997), *Bunny* (2001), *Portrait of My Lover as a Horse* (2002), *Lou-Lou* (2004) and *Red Roses* (2006). Her latest collections from Bloodaxe are *The Hat* (2008); *Fruitcake* (2009); *People Who Like Meatballs* (2012), shortlisted for both the Forward Poetry Prize and the Costa Poetry Award; *The Sparkling Jewel of Naturism* (2014); *Jutland* (2015), shortlisted for both the T.S. Eliot Prize and the Roehampton Poetry Prize; and *The Magnitude of My Sublime Existence* (2016).

Violet was a Poetry Book Society Choice and was shortlisted for all three of the UK's major poetry prizes, the Forward Prize, T.S. Eliot Prize and Whitbread Poetry Award. *Bunny* won the Whitbread Poetry Award, was a Poetry Book Society Choice and was shortlisted for the T.S. Eliot Prize. *Lou-Lou* and *The Hat* were Poetry Book Society Recommendations, while *Jutland* was a Special Commendation. She was given a Cholmondeley Award in 1986 and a University of East Anglia Writing Fellowship in 1991, and was a Royal Literary Fund Fellow at the University of Exeter in 2003-06.

As a tutor, Selima Hill has worked in prisons, hospitals and monasteries as well as for the Arvon Foundation, the Poetry School and London's Southbank Centre. She has worked on several collaborations with artists including: *Parched Swallows* with choreographer Emily Claid; *Point of Entry* with sculptor Bill Woodrow; and *Trembling Hearts in the Bodies of Rocks* with performance artist Ilona Medved-Lost.